ESSENTIAL ELEMENTS

FOR BAND

COMPREHENSIVE BAND METHOD

TIM LAUTZENHEISER   **JOHN HIGGINS**   **CHARLES MENGHINI**
PAUL LAVENDER   **TOM C. RHODES**   **DON BIERSCHENK**

Band is… **M**aking music with a family of lifelong friends.
Understanding how commitment and dedication lead to success.
Sharing the joy and rewards of working together.
Individuals who develop self-confidence.
Creativity—expressing yourself in a universal language.
Band is…**MUSIC!**

Strike up the band,
Tim Lautzenheiser

Flutes were known to exist in ancient civilizations. Over the years, they have been made of wood or metal. Early flutes, such as recorders, are played pointing forward. The other type of flute, called a transverse flute until the mid-1800s, is played to the side.

In 1847, Theobald Boehm designed the modern flute. This flute is capable of playing with more volume than older flutes. The keys Mr. Boehm added also allow the instrument to play a full chromatic scale, and help it to play better in tune.

The flute family includes the C Flute (the most common), C Piccolo, Alto and Bass Flutes. As the highest pitched members of the concert band, marching band and orchestra, flutes play melodies, harmonies and solos, and are important members of the woodwind family.

J. S. Bach, Claude Debussy and Ralph Vaughan Williams are important composers who have written music for the flute. Some famous flute performers are Louis Moyse and James Galway.

To create an account, visit:
www.essentialelementsinteractive.com

Student Activation Code
E1FL-9058-5587-0224

ISBN 978-0-634-00311-0
Copyright © 2004 by HAL LEONARD CORPORATION
International Copyright Secured   All Rights Reserved

HAL•LEONARD®
CORPORATION

7777 W. BLUEMOUND RD. P.O. BOX 13819 MILWAUKEE, WI 53213

THE BASICS

Posture

Sit on the edge of your chair, and always keep your:
- Spine straight and tall
- Shoulders back and relaxed
- Feet flat on the floor

Breathing & Airstream

Breathing is a natural thing we all do constantly. To discover the correct airstream to play your instrument:
- Place the palm of your hand near your mouth.
- Inhale deeply through the corners of your mouth, keeping your shoulders steady. Your waist should expand like a balloon.
- Slowly whisper "too" as you gradually exhale air into your palm.

The air you feel is the airstream. It produces sound through the instrument. Your tongue is like a faucet or valve that releases the airstream.

Producing The Essential Tone

Embouchure (ahm´-bah-shure) is your mouth's position on the mouthpiece of the instrument. A good embouchure takes time and effort, so carefully follow these steps for success:

- Hold the closed end of the head joint in your left hand. Cover the open end with the palm of your right hand.
- Rest the embouchure plate on your bottom lip. Center the embouchure hole on the center of your lips. Check by touching the embouchure hole with the tip of your tongue.
- Gently roll the head joint forward so that approximately 1/4 of the embouchure hole is covered by the lower lip.
- Keep upper and lower teeth spaced slightly apart.
- Draw the corners of your mouth straight back and relax your lower lip.
- Make a small opening in the center of your lips. Blow air partly into and partly across the embouchure hole.
- Practice regularly in front of a mirror. Roll the head joint in or out to find the embouchure position that produces your best clear and full tone.

Taking Care Of Your Instrument

Before putting your instrument back in its case after playing, do the following:
- Carefully remove the head joint and shake any water out.
- Put a clean soft cloth on the end of your cleaning rod and swab out the head joint.
- Twist the middle and foot joints apart and draw the cleaning rod through each joint.
- Carefully wipe the outside of each section to keep the finish clean.

MOUTHPIECE WORKOUT

Form your embouchure and take a deep breath without raising your shoulders. Whisper "too" and gradually exhale your full airstream. Strive for an even tone.

"too"

REST

"too"

REST

Getting It Together

Step 1 Hold the head joint in your left hand and the middle joint in your right hand. Gently twist and insert the head joint into the middle joint. Make sure that the embouchure hole is directly in line with the middle joint's row of keys.

Step 2 Hold the assembled middle joint in your left hand and the foot joint in your right hand. Gently twist and insert the middle joint into the foot joint. The embouchure hole, keys of the middle joint and the long rod on the foot joint should all line up.

Step 3 Rest your left thumb on the underside's long straight key. Keep your wrist straight. Your fingers should arch naturally. Rest your fingertips on the center of the keys.

Step 4 Place the tip of your right thumb on the flute's underside between your first and second fingers. Arch your fingers and rest them lightly on the keys. Put your little finger on the E-flat key.

Step 5 Allow the embouchure plate to press lightly against your lower lip. Hold the flute as shown:

READING MUSIC

Identify and draw each of these symbols:

Music Staff

The **music staff** has 5 lines and 4 spaces where notes and rests are written.

Ledger Lines

Ledger lines extend the music staff. Notes on ledger lines can be above or below the staff.

Measures & Bar Lines

Measure   *Measure*

Bar Line   *Bar Line*   *Bar Line*

Bar lines divide the music staff into **measures**.

Long Tone

To begin, we'll use a special "Long Tone" note. Hold the tone until your teacher tells you to rest. Practice long tones each day to develop your sound.

1. THE FIRST NOTE

Hold each long tone until your teacher tells you to rest.

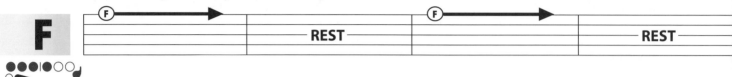

F

△ To play "F," place your fingers on the keys as shown.

The Beat

The **beat** is the pulse of music, and like your heartbeat it should remain very steady. Counting aloud and foot-tapping help us maintain a steady beat. Tap your foot **down** on each number and **up** on each "&."

One beat = 1 &
            ↓   ↑

Notes And Rests

Notes tell us how high or low to play by their placement on a line or space of the music staff, and how long to play by their shape. **Rests** tell us to count silent beats.

♩	Quarter Note	= 1 beat
⅔	Quarter Rest	= 1 silent beat

2. COUNT AND PLAY

| Count: | 1 | & | 2 | & | 3 | & | 4 | & | 1 | & | 2 | & | 3 | & | 4 | & | 1 | & | 2 | & | 3 | & | 4 | & | 1 | & | 2 | & | 3 | & | 4 | & |
| Tap: | ↓ | ↑ | ↓ | ↑ | ↓ | ↑ | ↓ | ↑ | ↓ | ↑ | ↓ | ↑ | ↓ | ↑ | ↓ | ↑ | ↓ | ↑ | ↓ | ↑ | ↓ | ↑ | ↓ | ↑ | ↓ | ↑ | ↓ | ↑ | ↓ | ↑ | ↓ | ↑ |

3. A NEW NOTE

Look for the fingering diagram under each new note. This note is "E♭ (E-flat)."

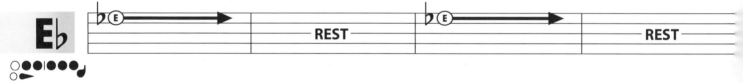

E♭

4. TWO'S A TEAM

| Count & Tap: | 1 | & | 2 | & | 3 | & | 4 | & | 1 | & | 2 | & | 3 | & | 4 | & | 1 | & | 2 | & | 3 | & | 4 | & | 1 | & | 2 | & | 3 | & | 4 | & |

5. HEADING DOWN

Practice long tones on each new note.

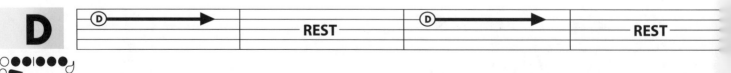

D

6. MOVING ON UP

| Count & Tap: | 1 | & | 2 | & | 3 | & | 4 | & | 1 | & | 2 | & | 3 | & | 4 | & | 1 | & | 2 | & | 3 | & | 4 | & | 1 | & | 2 | & | 3 | & | 4 | & |

Double Bar ⟶ indicates the end of a piece of music.

Repeat Sign ⟶ Without stopping, play once again from the beginning.

7. THE LONG HAUL *Double Bar*

C

8. FOUR BY FOUR *Repeat Sign*

Count & Tap: 1 & 2 & 3 & 4 &   1 & 2 & 3 & 4 &   1 & 2 & 3 & 4 &   1 & 2 & 3 & 4 &

9. TOUCHDOWN

B♭

10. THE FAB FIVE

1 & 2 & 3 & 4 &   1 & 2 & 3 & 4 &   1 & 2 & 3 & 4 &   1 & 2 & 3 & 4 &

Treble Clef
(G Clef) indicates the position of note names on a music staff: Second line is G.

Time Signature indicates how many beats per measure and what kind of note gets one beat.

$\frac{4}{4}$ = **4 beats** per measure
= **Quarter** note gets one beat

Note Names
Each note is on a line or space of the staff. These note names are indicated by the Treble Clef.

THEORY

Sharp ♯ raises the note and remains in effect for the entire measure.

Flat ♭ lowers the note and remains in effect for the entire measure.

Natural ♮ cancels a flat (♭) or sharp (♯) and remains in effect for the entire measure.

11. READING THE NOTES *Compare this to exercise 10, THE FAB FIVE.*

1 & 2 & 3 & 4 &   1 & 2 & 3 & 4 &   1 & 2 & 3 & 4 &   1 & 2 & 3 & 4 &

12. FIRST FLIGHT

13. ESSENTIAL ELEMENTS QUIZ *Fill in the remaining note names before playing.*

B♭ C D

Whole Note

o ——→ = 4 Beats

1 & 2 & 3 & 4 &

Whole Rest

= A Whole Measure of Silent Beats

1 & 2 & 3 & 4 &

Whole Rest hangs from a staff line.

Half Rest sits on a staff line.

0. RHYTHM RAP *Clap the rhythm while counting and tapping.*

Clap

1 & 2 & 3 & 4 &   1 & 2 & 3 & 4 &   1 & 2 & 3 & 4 &   1 & 2 & 3 & 4 &   1 & 2 & 3 & 4 &   1 & 2 & 3 & 4 &

1. THE WHOLE THING

1 & 2 & 3 & 4 &   1 & 2 & 3 & 4 &   1 & 2 & 3 & 4 &   1 & 2 & 3 & 4 &   1 & 2 & 3 & 4 &   1 & 2 & 3 & 4 &

Duet A composition with two different parts, played together.

2. SPLIT DECISION – Duet

Key Signature The **Key Signature** tells us which notes to play with sharps ($\sharp$) or flats ($\flat$) throughout the music. Your Key Signature indicates the *Key of B♭* – play all B's as B-flats, and E's as E-flats.

THEORY

3. MARCH STEPS

△ *Play B♭'s and E♭'s*

4. LISTEN TO OUR SECTIONS

Percussion   Woodwinds   Brass   Percussion   Woodwinds   Brass   Perc.   Ww.   Brass   All

5. LIGHTLY ROW

6. ESSENTIAL ELEMENTS QUIZ *Draw in the bar lines before you play.*

8

      Hold the note (or rest) longer than normal.

27. REACHING HIGHER – New Note
Practice long tones on each new note.

Fermata

28. AU CLAIRE DE LA LUNE
French Folk Song

29. REMIX

Harmony
Two or more notes played together. Each combination forms a *chord*.

30. LONDON BRIDGE – Duet
English Folk Song

Austrian composer **Wolfgang Amadeus Mozart** (1756–1791) was a child prodigy who started playing professionally at age six, and lived during the time of the American Revolution. Mozart's music is melodic and imaginative. He wrote more than 600 compositions during his short life, including a piano piece based on the famous song, "Twinkle, Twinkle, Little Star."

31. A MOZART MELODY
Adaptation

32. ESSENTIAL ELEMENTS QUIZ
Draw these symbols where they belong and write in the note names before you play:

9

33. DEEP POCKETS – New Note

34. DOODLE ALL DAY

35. JUMP ROPE

Pick-Up Notes

One or more notes that come before the first *full* measure. The beats of Pick-Up Notes are subtracted from the last measure.

36. A-TISKET, A-TASKET

Dynamics

f – *forte* (play loudly) mf – *mezzo forte* (play moderately loud) p – *piano* (play softly)

Remember to use full breath support to control your tone at all dynamic levels.

37. LOUD AND SOFT

38. JINGLE BELLS   *Keep your fingers close to the keys, curved naturally.*   J. S. Pierpont

39. MY DREYDL   *Use full breath support at all dynamic levels.*   Traditional Hanukkah Song

10

Eighth Notes

Each Eighth Note = ½ Beat
2 Eighth Notes = 1 Beat
Play on down and up taps.

1 &

1 & 2 &

Two or more Eighth Notes have a *beam* across the stems.

▼ *Beam*

=

40. RHYTHM RAP *Clap the rhythm while counting and tapping.*

41. EIGHTH NOTE JAM

42. SKIP TO MY LOU

American Folk Song

43. LONG, LONG AGO *Good posture improves your sound. Always sit straight and tall.*

44. OH, SUSANNA

Stephen Collins Foster

HISTORY

Italian composer **Gioacchino Rossini** (1792–1868) began composing as a teenager and was very proficient on the piano, viola and horn. He wrote "William Tell" at age 37 as the last of his forty operas, and its familiar theme is still heard today on radio and television.

45. ESSENTIAL ELEMENTS QUIZ — WILLIAM TELL

Gioacchino Rossini

$\frac{2}{4}$ Time Signature

= **2 beats** per measure
= **Quarter** note gets one beat

Conducting

Practice conducting this two-beat pattern.

46. RHYTHM RAP

Clap

1 & 2 & 1 & 2 & 1 & 2 & 1 & 2 & 1 & 2 & 1 & 2 & 1 & 2 & 1 & 2 &

7. TWO BY TWO

1 & 2 & 1 & 2 & 1 & 2 & 1 & 2 & 1 & 2 & 1 & 2 & 1 & 2 & 1 & 2 &

Tempo Markings

Tempo is the speed of music. Tempo markings are usually written above the staff, in Italian.

Allegro – Fast tempo   **Moderato** – Medium tempo   **Andante** – Slower walking tempo

8. HIGH SCHOOL CADETS – March

John Philip Sousa

Reproduced by Permission of Boosey & Hawkes Music Publishers Ltd.

9. HEY, HO! NOBODY'S HOME – New Note

Dynamics

Crescendo (gradually louder)   *Decrescendo* or *Diminuendo* (gradually softer)

). CLAP THE DYNAMICS

. PLAY THE DYNAMICS

PERFORMANCE SPOTLIGHT

52. PERFORMANCE WARM-UPS

TONE BUILDER

RHYTHM ETUDE

RHYTHM RAP

CHORALE

53. AURA LEE – Duet or Band Arrangement

(Part A = Melody, Part B = Harmony)

George R. Poult

54. FRÈRE JACQUES – Round   *(When group A reaches ②, group B begins at ①)*

French Folk S

PERFORMANCE SPOTLIGHT

5. WHEN THE SAINTS GO MARCHING IN – Band Arrangement

Arr. by John Higgins

6. OLD MACDONALD HAD A BAND – Section Feature

7. ODE TO JOY (from Symphony No. 9)

Ludwig van Beethoven
Arr. by John Higgins

8. HARD ROCK BLUES – Encore

John Higgins

14

| Tie | A curved line connecting notes of the same pitch. Play one note for the combined counts of the tied notes. | = 2 Beats |

59. FIT TO BE TIED

2 beats △

60. ALOUETTE

French-Canadian Folk Son

3 beats △

Dotted Half Note

 = 3 Beats
1 & 2 & 3 &

 Dot
A dot adds half the value of the note.

2 beats + 1 beat = 3 beats

61. ALOUETTE – THE SEQUEL

French-Canadian Folk Son

HISTORY American composer **Stephen Collins Foster** (1826–1864) was born near Pittsburgh, PA. He has become the most recognized song writer of his time for works such as "Oh Susanna," which became popular during the California Gold Rush of 1849. Among his most well-known songs are "My Old Kentucky Home" and "Camptown Races."

62. CAMPTOWN RACES

Stephen Collins Fost

63. NEW DIRECTIONS – New Note
To play lower notes, blow softly and direct the airstream lower into the embouchure ho

F

64. THE NOBLES
Always use a full airstream. Keep fingers above the keys, curved naturally.

3 beats △

65. ESSENTIAL ELEMENTS QUIZ

$\frac{3}{4}$ Time Signature

$\frac{3}{4}$ = **3 beats** per measure
= **Quarter** note gets one beat

Conducting

Practice conducting this three-beat pattern.

66. RHYTHM RAP

Clap

1 & 2 & 3 &   1 & 2 & 3 &   1 & 2 & 3 &   1 & 2 & 3 &   1 & 2 & 3 &   1 & 2 & 3 &   1 & 2 & 3 &   1 & 2 & 3 &

67. THREE BEAT JAM

1 & 2 & 3 &   1 & 2 & 3 &   1 & 2 & 3 &   1 & 2 & 3 &   1 & 2 & 3 &   1 & 2 & 3 &   1 & 2 & 3 &   1 & 2 & 3 &

68. BARCAROLLE

Jacques Offenbach

Moderato

mf

HISTORY

Norwegian composer **Edvard Grieg** (1843–1907) wrote *Peer Gynt Suite* for a play by Henrik Ibsen in 1875, the year before the telephone was invented by Alexander Graham Bell. "Morning" is a melody from *Peer Gynt Suite*. Music used in plays, or in films and television, is called **incidental music**.

69. MORNING (from Peer Gynt)

Edvard Grieg

Andante

p   *mf*   *p*

Accent — Emphasize the note.

70. ACCENT YOUR TALENT

Clap

HISTORY

Latin American music has its roots in the African, Native American, Spanish and Portuguese cultures. This diverse music features lively accompaniments by drums and other percussion instruments such as maracas and claves. Music from Latin America continues to influence jazz, classical and popular styles of music. "Chiapanecas" is a popular children's dance and game song.

71. MEXICAN CLAPPING SONG ("Chiapanecas")

Latin American Folk Song

f

72. ESSENTIAL CREATIVITY

Compose your own music for measures 3 and 4 using this rhythm:

THEORY

Accidental

Any sharp, flat or natural sign which appears in the music without being in the key signature is called an **accidental**.

Flat ♭

A **flat** sign lowers the pitch of a note by a half-step. The note A-flat sounds a half-step below A, and all A's become A-flats for the rest of the measure where they occur.

73. HOT MUFFINS – New Note

Flat applies to all A's in measure.

74. COSSACK DANCE

75. BASIC BLUES – New Note

Flat applies to all A's in measure.

THEORY

New Key Signature

This Key Signature indicates the *Key of E♭* – play all B's as B-flats, all E's as E-flats, and all A's as A-flats.

1st & 2nd Endings

Play through the 1st Ending. Then play the repeated section of music, **skipping** the 1st Ending and playing the 2nd Ending.

76. HIGH FLYING

HISTORY

Japanese folk music actually has its origins in ancient China. "Sakura, Sakura" was performed on instruments such as the **koto**, a 13-string instrument that is more than 4000 years old, and the **shakuhachi** or bamboo flute. The unique sound of this ancient Japanese melody results from the pentatonic (or five-note) sequence used in this tonal system.

77. SAKURA, SAKURA – Band Arrangement

Japanese Folk So
Arr. by John Higg

78. UP ON A HOUSETOP

79. JOLLY OLD ST. NICK – Duet

See page 9 for additional holiday music, MY DREYDL and JINGLE BELLS.

80. THE BIG AIRSTREAM – New Note

81. WALTZ THEME (THE MERRY WIDOW WALTZ)

Franz Lehar

82. AIR TIME

83. DOWN BY THE STATION

84. ESSENTIAL ELEMENTS QUIZ

85. ESSENTIAL CREATIVITY *Using these notes, improvise your own rhythms:*

DAILY WARM-UPS

WORK-OUTS FOR TONE & TECHNIQUE

86. TONE BUILDER *Use a steady stream of air.*

87. RHYTHM BUILDER

88. TECHNIQUE TRAX

89. CHORALE *(Adapted from Cantata 147)*

Johann Sebastian Bach

THEORY

Theme and Variations

A musical form featuring a **theme**, or primary melody, followed by **variations**, or altered versions of the theme.

90. VARIATIONS ON A FAMILIAR THEME

D.C. al Fine

At the **D.C. al Fine** play again from the beginning, stopping at **Fine** *(fee'- nay)*.
D.C. is the abbreviation for **Da Capo**, or "to the beginning," and **Fine** means "the end."

91. BANANA BOAT SONG

Caribbean Folk So

Natural ♮ A **natural** sign cancels a flat (♭) or sharp (♯) and remains in effect for the entire measure.

92. RAZOR'S EDGE – New Note

△ E♮

93. THE MUSIC BOX

Moderato

p   △ E

African-American spirituals originated in the 1700's, midway through the period of slavery in the United States. One of the largest categories of true American folk music, these primarily religious songs were sung and passed on for generations without being written down. The first collection of spirituals was published in 1867, four years after The Emancipation Proclamation was signed into law.

94. EZEKIEL SAW THE WHEEL

Allegro

African-American Spiritual

Slur A curved line which connects notes of different pitch. Tongue only the first note in a **slur**.

95. SMOOTH OPERATOR

△ *Slur 2 notes – tongue only the first.*

96. GLIDING ALONG

△ *Slur 4 notes – tongue only the first.*

Ragtime is an American music style that was popular from the 1890's until the time of World War I. This early form of jazz brought fame to pianists like "Jelly Roll" Morton and Scott Joplin, who wrote "The Entertainer" and "Maple Leaf Rag." Surprisingly, the style was incorporated into some orchestral music by Igor Stravinsky and Claude Debussy. The trombones now learn to play a *glissando,* a technique used in ragtime and other styles of music.

97. TROMBONE RAG

Allegro

98. ESSENTIAL ELEMENTS QUIZ

Andante

99. TAKE THE LEAD – New Note

THEORY

Phrase

A musical "sentence" which is often 2 or 4 measures long. Try to play a **phrase** in one breath.

100. THE COLD WIND

101. PHRASEOLOGY *Write in the breath mark(s) between the phrases.*

THEORY

New Key Signature

This **Key Signature** indicates the *Key of F* – play all B's as B-flats.

Multiple Measure Rest

The number above the staff tells you how many full measures to rest. Count each measure of rest in sequence:

102. SATIN LATIN

HISTORY

German composer **Johann Sebastian Bach** (1685–1750) was part of a large family of famous musicians and became the most recognized composer of the Baroque era. Beginning as a choir member, Bach soon became an organist, a teacher, and a prolific composer, writing more than 600 masterworks. This *Minuet*, or dance in 3/4 time, was written as a teaching piece for use with an early form of the piano.

103. MINUET – Duet

Johann Sebastian Bach

104. ESSENTIAL CREATIVITY *This melody can be played in 3/4 or 4/4. Pencil in either time signature, draw the bar lines and play. Now erase the bar lines and try the other time signature. Do the phrases sound different?*

105. NATURALLY

Austrian composer **Franz Peter Schubert** (1797–1828) lived a shorter life than any other great composer, but he created an incredible amount of music: more than 600 art-songs (concert music for voice and accompaniment), ten symphonies, chamber music, operas, choral works and piano pieces. His "March Militaire" was originally a piano duet.

106. MARCH MILITAIRE – New Note

Franz Schubert

107. THE FLAT ZONE – New Note

08. ON TOP OF OLD SMOKEY

American Folk Song

Boogie-woogie is a style of the **blues**, and it was first recorded by pianist Clarence "Pine Top" Smith in 1928, one year after Charles Lindbergh's solo flight across the Atlantic. A form of jazz, blues music features altered notes and is usually written in 12-measure verses, like "Bottom Bass Boogie."

09. BOTTOM BASS BOOGIE – Duet

PERFORMANCE SPOTLIGHT

Solo with Piano Accompaniment

You can perform this solo with or without a piano accompanist. Play it for the band, the school or your family. It is part of **Symphony No. 9 ("From The New World")** by Czech composer **Antonin Dvořák** (1841–1904). He wrote it while visiting America in 1893, and was inspired to include melodies from American folksongs and spirituals. This is the **Largo** (or "very slow tempo") theme.

8. THEME FROM "NEW WORLD SYMPHONY"

Antonin Dvořák

no Accompaniment

Great musicians give encouragement to fellow performers. On this page, clarinetists learn their instruments' upper register in the "Grenadilla Gorilla Jumps" (named after the grenadilla wood used to make clarinets). Brass players learn lip slurs, a new warm-up pattern. The success of your band depends on everyone's effort and encouragement.

119. GRENADILLA GORILLA JUMP No. 1

120. JUMPIN' UP AND DOWN

121. GRENADILLA GORILLA JUMP No. 2 – New Note

C

➤ *Higher notes are easier when you aim your airstream higher across the embouchure hole.*

122. JUMPIN' FOR JOY

123. GRENADILLA GORILLA JUMP No. 3

124. JUMPIN' JACKS

THEORY

Interval

The distance between two pitches is an **interval**. Starting with "1" on the lower note, count each line and space between the notes. The number of the higher note is the distance of the interval.

125. ESSENTIAL ELEMENTS QUIZ *Write in the numbers of the intervals, counting up from the lower notes.*

Intervals: 2nd

126. GRENADILLA GORILLA JUMP No. 4

127. THREE IS THE COUNT

128. GRENADILLA GORILLA JUMP No. 5

129. TECHNIQUE TRAX

130. CROSSING OVER

Trio

A **trio** is a composition with three parts played together. Practice this trio with two other players and listen for the 3-part harmony.

131. KUM BAH YAH – Trio   *Always check the key signature.*

African Folk Song

26

Repeat Signs

Repeat the section of music enclosed by the **repeat signs**. (If 1st and 2nd endings are used, they are played as usual — but go back only to the first repeat sign, not to the beginning.)

132. MICHAEL ROW THE BOAT ASHORE — African-American Spiritual

Andante

133. AUSTRIAN WALTZ — Austrian Folk Song

Moderato

134. BOTANY BAY — Australian Folk Song

Allegro

THEORY

C Time Signature
C = **Common Time** (Same as 4/4)

Conducting
Practice conducting this four-beat pattern.

135. TECHNIQUE TRAX *Practice at all dynamic levels.*

136. FINLANDIA — Jean Sibeliu

Andante

© Breitkopf & Haertel, Wiesbaden - Leip

137. ESSENTIAL CREATIVITY
Create your own variations by penciling in a dot and a flag to change the rhythm of any measure from ♩ ♩ *to* ♩. ♪

138. EASY GORILLA JUMPS

139. TECHNIQUE TRAX *Always check the key signature.*

140. MORE TECHNIQUE TRAX

141. GERMAN FOLK SONG

142. THE SAINTS GO MARCHIN' AGAIN

James Black and Katherine Purvis

143. LOWLAND GORILLA WALK

144. SMOOTH SAILING

145. MORE GORILLA JUMPS

146. FULL COVERAGE

28

THEORY

Scale

A **scale** is a sequence of notes in ascending or descending order. Like a musical "ladder," each step is the next consecutive note in the key. This scale is in your Key of B♭ (two flats), so the top and bottom notes are both B♭'s. The interval between the B♭'s is an octave.

147. CONCERT B♭ SCALE

THEORY

Chord & Arpeggio

When two or more notes are played together, they form a **chord** or **harmony**. This B♭ chord is built from the 1st, 3rd and 5th steps of the B♭ scale. The 8th step is the same as the 1st, but it is an octave higher. An **arpeggio** is a "broken" chord whose notes are played individually.

148. IN HARMONY
Divide the notes of the chords between band members and play together. Does the arpeggio sound like a chord?

149. SCALE AND ARPEGGIO

HISTORY

Austrian composer **Franz Josef Haydn** (1732–1809) wrote 104 symphonies. Many of these works had nicknames and included brilliant, unique effects for their time. His Symphony No. 94 was named "The Surprise Symphony" because the soft second movement included a sudden loud dynamic, intended to wake up an often sleepy audience. Pay special attention to dynamics when you play this famous theme.

150. THEME FROM "SURPRISE SYMPHONY"
Franz Josef Haydn

151. ESSENTIAL ELEMENTS QUIZ – THE STREETS OF LAREDO
American Folk Song

Write in the note names before you play.

PERFORMANCE SPOTLIGHT

152. SCHOOL SPIRIT – Band Arrangement

W.T. Purdy
Arr. by John Higgins

Soli

When playing music marked **Soli**, you are part of a group "solo" or group feature. Listen carefully in "Carnival of Venice," and name the instruments that play the Soli part at each indicated measure number.

53. CARNIVAL OF VENICE – Band Arrangement

Julius Benedict
Arr. by John Higgins

⅃ DAILY WARM-UPS

WORK-OUTS FOR TONE & TECHNIQUE

154. RANGE AND FLEXIBILITY BUILDER

155. TECHNIQUE TRAX

156. CHORALE

Johann Sebastian Bach

HISTORY

The traditional Hebrew melody "Hatikvah" has been Israel's national anthem since the nation's inception. At the Declaration of State in 1948, it was sung by the gathered assembly during the opening ceremony and played by members of the Palestine Symphony Orchestra at its conclusion.

157. HATIKVAH

Israeli National Anthem

Eighth Note & Eighth Rest

♪ = 1/2 beat of sound

𝄾 = 1/2 beat of silence

1 & 2 &   1 & 2 &

158. RHYTHM RAP

1 & 2 & 1 & 2 & 1 & 2 & 1 & 2 & 1 & 2 & 1 & 2 & 1 & 2 & 1 & 2 &

159. EIGHTH NOTE MARCH

1 & 2 & 1 & 2 & 1 & 2 & 1 & 2 & 1 & 2 & 1 & 2 & 1 & 2 & 1 & 2 &

160. MINUET

Johann Sebastian Bach

161. RHYTHM RAP

1 & 2 & 3 & 4 & 1 & 2 & 3 & 4 & 1 & 2 & 3 & 4 & 1 & 2 & 3 & 4 &

162. EIGHTH NOTES OFF THE BEAT

1 & 2 & 3 & 4 & 1 & 2 & 3 & 4 & 1 & 2 & 3 & 4 & 1 & 2 & 3 & 4 &

163. EIGHTH NOTE SCRAMBLE

164. ESSENTIAL ELEMENTS QUIZ

32

165. DANCING MELODY – New Note

166. EL CAPITAN

John Philip Sous

Reproduced by Permission of Boosey & Hawkes Music Publishers

167. O CANADA

Calixa Lavalle
l'Hon. Judge Routhi
and Justice R.S. We

168. ESSENTIAL ELEMENTS QUIZ – METER MANIA *Count and clap before playing. Can you conduct this?*

Enharmonics

Two notes that are written differently, but sound the same (and played with the same fingering) are called **enharmonics**. Your fingering chart on pages 46–47 shows the fingerings for the enharmonic notes on your instrument.

On a piano keyboard, each black key is both a flat and a sharp:

169. SNAKE CHARMER   *Enharmonic notes use the same fingering.*

170. DARK SHADOWS

171. CLOSE ENCOUNTERS   *Enharmonic notes use the same fingering.*

172. MARCH SLAV

Peter Illyich Tchaikovsky

173. NOTES IN DISGUISE

Chromatic Notes

Chromatic notes are altered with sharps, flats and natural signs which are not in the key signature. The smallest distance between two notes is a half-step, and a scale made up of consecutive half-steps is called a **chromatic scale**.

174. HALF-STEPPIN'

34

HISTORY

French composer **Camille Saint-Saëns** (1835–1921) wrote music for virtually every medium: operas, suites, symphonies and chamber works. The "Egyptian Dance" is one of the main themes from his famous opera *Samson et Delilah*. The opera was written in the same year that Thomas Edison invented the phonograph—1877.

175. EGYPTIAN DANCE *Watch for enharmonics.*

Camille Saint-Saëns

176. SILVER MOON BOAT

Chinese Folk Song

HISTORY

German composer **Ludwig van Beethoven** (1770–1827) is considered to be one of the world's greatest composers, despite becoming completely deaf in 1802. Although he could not hear his music the way we can, he could "hear" it in his mind. As a testament to his greatness, his Symphony No. 9 (p. 13) was performed as the finale to the ceremony celebrating the reunification of Germany in 1990. This is the theme from his Symphony No. 7, second movement.

177. THEME FROM SYMPHONY NO. 7 – Duet

Ludwig van Beethoven

Russian composer **Peter Illyich Tchaikovsky** (1840–1893) wrote six symphonies and hundreds of other works including *The Nutcracker* ballet. He was a master at writing brilliant settings of folk music, and his original melodies are among the most popular of all time. His *1812 Overture* and *Capriccio Italien* were both written in 1880, the year after Thomas Edison developed the practical electric light bulb.

178. CAPRICCIO ITALIEN *Always check the key signature.* Peter Illyich Tchaikovsky

179. AMERICAN PATROL F.W. Meacham

180. WAYFARING STRANGER African-American Spiritual

181. ESSENTIAL ELEMENTS QUIZ – SCALE COUNTING CONQUEST

PERFORMANCE SPOTLIGHT

182. AMERICA THE BEAUTIFUL – Band Arrangement

Samuel A. Ward
Arr. by John Higgins

183. LA CUCARACHA – Band Arrangement

Latin American Folk Song
Arr. by John Higgins

PERFORMANCE SPOTLIGHT

184. THEME FROM 1812 OVERTURE – Band Arrangement

Peter Illyich Tchaikovsky
Arr. by John Higgins

PERFORMANCE SPOTLIGHT

Solo with Piano Accompaniment

Performing for an audience is an exciting part of being involved in music. This solo is based on *Serenade in G Major, K. 525*, also known as "Eine Kleine Nachtmusik" ("A Little Night Music"). **Wolfgang Amadeus Mozart** wrote this piece in 1787, the same year the American Constitution was signed into law. You and a piano accompanist can perform this for the band or at other school and community events.

185. EINE KLEINE NACHTMUSIK – Solo *(Concert E♭ version)*

Wolfgang Amadeus Mozart
Arr. by John Higgins

DUETS

Here is an opportunity to get together with a friend and enjoy playing music. The other player does not have to play the same instrument as you. Try to exactly match each other's rhythm, pitch and tone quality. Eventually, it may begin to sound like the two parts are being played by one person! Later, try switching parts.

186. SWING LOW, SWEET CHARIOT – Duet

African-American Spiritual

87. LA BAMBA – Duet

Mexican Folk Song

RUBANK® SCALE AND ARPEGGIO STUDIES

KEY OF B♭ *In this key signature, play all B♭'s and E♭'s.*

RUBANK® SCALE AND ARPEGGIO STUDIES

KEY OF F   *In this key signature, play all B♭'s.*

1.

2.

3.

4.

KEY OF A♭   *In this key signature, play all B♭'s, E♭'s, A♭'s and D♭'s.*

1.

2.

3.

4.

RHYTHM STUDIES

RHYTHM STUDIES

44

CREATING MUSIC

Composition

THEORY

Composition is the art of writing original music. A composer often begins by creating a melody made up of individual **phrases**, like short musical "sentences." Some melodies have phrases that seem to answer or respond to "question" phrases, as in Beethoven's *Ode To Joy*. Play this melody and listen to how phrases 2 and 4 give slightly different answers to the same question (phrases 1 and 3).

1. ODE TO JOY

Ludwig van Beethoven

2. Q. AND A. *Write your own "answer" phrases in this melody.*

3. PHRASE BUILDERS *Write 4 different phrases using the rhythms below each staff.*

4. YOU NAME IT: _____

Pick phrase A, B, C, or D from above, and write it as the "Question" for phrases 1 and 3 below. Then write 2 different "Answers" for phrases 2 and

Improvisation

THEORY

Improvisation is the art of freely creating your own melody *as you play.* Use these notes to play your own melody (Line A), to go with the accompaniment (Line B).

5. INSTANT MELODY

You can mark your progress through the book on this page. Fill in the stars as instructed by your band director.

ESSENTIAL ELEMENTS

STAR ACHIEVER

NAME_____

1. Page 2–3, The Basics
2. Page 5, EE Quiz, No. 13
3. Page 6, EE Quiz, No. 19
4. Page 7, EE Quiz, No. 26
5. Page 8, EE Quiz, No. 32
6. Page 10, EE Quiz, No. 45
7. Page 12–13, Performance Spotlight
8. Page 14, EE Quiz, No. 65
9. Page 15, Essential Creativity, No. 72
10. Page 17, EE Quiz, No. 84
11. Page 17, Essential Creativity, No. 85
12. Page 19, EE Quiz, No. 98
13. Page 20, Essential Creativity, No. 104
14. Page 21, No. 109

15. Page 22, EE Quiz, No. 117
16. Page 23, Performance Spotlight
17. Page 24, EE Quiz, No. 125
18. Page 26, Essential Creativity, No. 137
19. Page 28, No. 149
20. Page 28, EE Quiz, No. 151
21. Page 29, Performance Spotlight
22. Page 31, EE Quiz, No. 164
23. Page 32, EE Quiz, No. 168
24. Page 33, No. 174
25. Page 35, EE Quiz, No. 181
26. Page 36, Performance Spotlight
27. Page 37, Performance Spotlight
28. Page 38, Performance Spotlight

MUSIC — AN ESSENTIAL ELEMENT OF LIFE

FINGERING CHART

*Instrument courtesy of
Yamaha Corporation of America,
Band and Orchestral Division*

○ = Open
● = Pressed down

The most common fingering appears
first when two fingerings are shown.

Instrument Care Reminders

Before putting your instrument back in its case after playing, do the following:

- Carefully remove the head joint.
- Put a clean soft cloth on the end of your cleaning rod and swab out the head joint.
- Twist the middle and foot joints apart and draw the cleaning rod through each joint.
- Carefully wipe the outside of each section to keep the finish clean.

FINGERING CHART

FLUTE

REFERENCE INDEX

Definitions (pg.)

Accent   15
Accidental   16
Allegro   11
Andante   11
Arpeggio   28
Bass Clef   5   (Bass clef inst.)
Bar Lines   3
Beat   4
Blues   21
Breath Mark   6
Chord   28
Chromatic Notes   33
Chromatic Scale   33
Common Time   26
Crescendo   11
D.C. al Fine   18
Decrescendo   11
Diminuendo   11
Dotted Half Note   14
Dotted Quarter Note   22
Double Bar   5
Duet   7
Dynamics   9
Eighth Note   10
Eighth Rest   31
Embouchure   2   (Brass & WW's)
Enharmonics   33
Fermata   8
1st & 2nd Endings   16
Flat   5
Forte (𝑓)   9
Glissando   19   (Trombone)
Half Note   6
Half-step   33
Harmony   8
Interval   24
Key Signature   7
Largo   23
Ledger Lines   3
Measure   3
Mezzo Forte (𝑚𝑓)   9
Moderato   11
Multiple Measure Rest   20
Music Staff   3
Natural Sign   5
Notes   4
Phrase   20
Piano (𝑝)   9
Pick-Up Notes   9
Quarter Note   4
Ragtime   19
Repeat Sign   5, 26
Rests   4, 6, 7, 31
Round (Canon)   12
Scale   28
Sharp   5

Slur   19
Soli   29
Solo   23, 38
Tempo   11
Theme And Variations   18
Tie   14
Time Signature   5
Treble Clef   5   (Treble clef inst.)
Trio   25
Whole Note   7

Composers

JOHANN SEBASTIAN BACH
• Chorale (from Cantata 147)   18
• Chorale   30
• Minuet   20
• Minuet   31
LUDWIG VAN BEETHOVEN
• Ode To Joy (from Sym. No. 9)   13
• Theme From Symphony No. 7   34
JOHANNES BRAHMS
• Theme From Sym. No. 1   38
   (Brass & Low WW's)
ANTONIN DVORÁK
• Theme From "New World Sym."   23
STEPHEN COLLINS FOSTER
• Camptown Races   14
• Oh, Susanna   10
EDVARD GRIEG
• Morning (from Peer Gynt)   15
FRANZ JOSEF HAYDN
• Theme From "Surprise Symphony"   28
FRANZ LEHAR
• Waltz Theme   17
WOLFGANG AMADEUS MOZART
• A Mozart Melody   8
• Eine Kleine Nachtmusik   38
   (High WW's)
JACQUES OFFENBACH
• Barcarolle   15
GIOACCHINO ROSSINI
• William Tell   10
CAMILLE SAINT-SAËNS
• Egyptian Dance   34
FRANZ SCHUBERT
• March Militaire   21
JEAN SIBELIUS
• Finlandia   26
JOHN PHILIP SOUSA
• El Capitan   32
• High School Cadets   11
PETER ILLYICH TCHAIKOVSKY
• Capriccio Italien   35
• March Slav   33
• 1812 Overture   37

World Music

AFRICAN
• Kum Bah Yah   25
AMERICAN
• American Patrol   35
• America The Beautiful   36
• Aura Lee   12
• Ezekiel Saw The Wheel   19
• Go Tell Aunt Rhodie   6
• Michael Row The Boat Ashore   26
• On Top Of Old Smokey   21
• Skip To My Lou   10
• Swing Low, Sweet Chariot   39
• The Streets Of Laredo   28
• Wayfaring Stranger   35
• When The Saints Go Marching In   13, 27
AUSTRALIAN
• Botany Bay   26
AUSTRIAN
• Austrian Waltz   26
CANADIAN
• Alouette   14
• O Canada   32
CARIBBEAN
• Banana Boat Song   18
CHINESE
• Silver Moon Boat   34
ENGLISH
• London Bridge   8
• Scarborough Fair   22
• Sea Chanty   22
FRENCH
• Au Claire De La Lune   8
• Frère Jacques   12
GERMAN
• German Folk Song   27
ISRAELI
• Hatikva   30
ITALIAN
• Carnival Of Venice   29
JAPANESE
• Sakura, Sakura   16
MEXICAN
• Chiapanecas   15
• La Bamba   39
• La Cucaracha   36
SCOTTISH
• Auld Lang Syne   22
TRADITIONAL HOLIDAY MUSIC
• Jingle Bells   9
• Jolly Old St. Nick   17
• My Dreydl   9
• Up On A Housetop   17